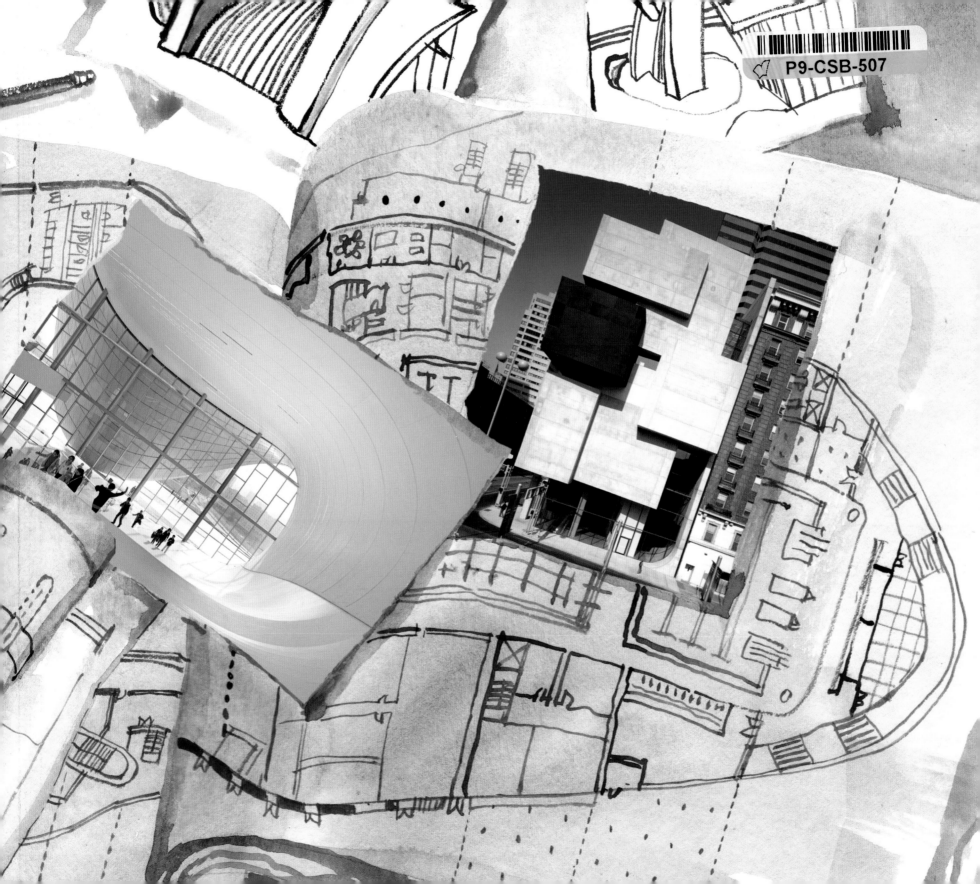

Building

"You really have to have a goal.

Zaha

The Story of Architect Zaha Hadid

The goal posts might shift, but you should have a goal."
— **Zaha Hadid**

VICTORIA TENTLER-KRYLOV

Orchard Books I Scholastic Inc. I New York

Zaha Hadid was a thinker and an observer and never remained still. As a young girl, she loved to explore the mosques and palaces around Baghdad, where sunlight streamed through windows, forming shadows that shifted and rippled like water.

Zaha loved to stay up late reading, and in one book she read about how people built floating homes in the Sumerian wetlands. She was determined to see this for herself! Zaha traveled with her father to Sumer, where watery marshes, reeds, and grasses rippled and flowed all around.

It was beautiful — complete harmony — and it never remained still. Zaha wondered whether it was better to live in a modern city like Baghdad, or like this, as one with nature.

One time, Zaha's aunt and uncle came over, excited to share a scale model of their future house. Zaha wasn't allowed to touch the model, but she couldn't pull herself away. It was a bit like a dollhouse, but it was much more than a toy! Thoughts of creating, shaping, and constructing danced in Zaha's head.

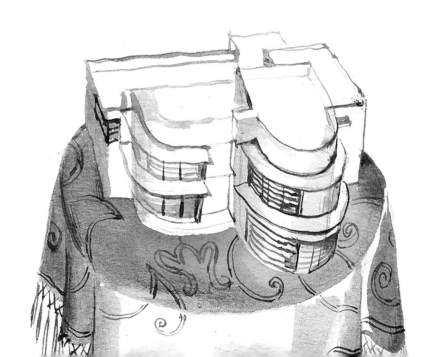

Zaha set a goal for herself and got to work right away. Her family could tell she had big plans. "You could become Iraq's first female astronaut!" one of her brothers suggested. But Zaha had something else in mind. "I want to be an architect," she announced. She was interested in exploring a different kind of space!

Construction sites fascinated Zaha — she couldn't pass one without stopping to imagine the shapes and structures that might emerge. When she didn't have her notebook to sketch in, she worked out calculations in her head. Zaha loved math — she didn't see much difference between solving problems and designing buildings. Both were creative and challenging, just what she liked! Zaha got her math degree in Beirut, then packed up and moved to London.

HOUSEHOLD GOODS

It was time to get serious about studying architecture. It rained and rained in England, but this didn't bother Zaha — she didn't have time to bask in the sun anyway! She stayed in the studio for hours on end, sketching, reading, and thinking.

Zaha was not afraid to question what was possible. Even her process was different. "The way she drew a staircase you would smash your head against the ceiling," said one of her professors. But Zaha knew she could always fix the details. And she was right. Zaha dreamed big and defied convention. She reached for paints and brushes and conjured structures that tilted, swayed, and floated on air.

Zaha impressed her
professors, and two of them hired
her to work at their firm after
graduation. Zaha brought new ideas
to the office in more ways than one. She
liked to challenge the rules, standing her
ground in fabulous, furry heels. "There's an
assumption that if you dress like a man, then
people will respond to you more," she stated.
"You shouldn't have to look drab to appear
professional."

After three years, Zaha opened her own studio, where she worked harder than ever. "I think about architecture all the time . . . I dream it sometimes," she said. Zaha was becoming famous in England — people talked about her unconventional ideas and her paintings – and yet, she wasn't hired to design!

So Zaha started entering competitions. One contest was for a hotel and sports club in Hong Kong. She painted the whole island, with her design nestled right among its mountains. Zaha called it "a confetti snowstorm" and her innovation launched her to first place, beating out many prominent architects! But the organizers decided the design was too complicated to build, and dropped the project. Though Zaha won, the goalpost had moved.

Zaha wasn't deterred. She kept working and one day a
client from Germany called: Could Zaha design a fire station? Yes!
She decided to make the building look like a bird taking flight. People
couldn't believe how daring it was, and showered Zaha with praise.
At last, one of Zaha's designs had become reality!

Success came with even more scrutiny. Zaha continued to get work, yet critics insisted she was in danger of becoming a "paper architect" — someone whose designs stay on paper and never get built. Was this really about her designs, or was it because she was different and challenged what was possible? Zaha often didn't agree with the criticism she received, so she had to be tougher than most and confident in her vision.

Θn to the next challenge! Zaha was hired to create a housing complex in Austria on a complicated setting with many obstacles that overlapped and intertwined! As Zaha sketched, she remembered the marshes she visited as a child. She pictured the rippling harmony between the man-made structures, the reeds, the water, and the wind.

Could she approach this project the same way? Was it possible to create complete harmony in a space so divided? Zaha came up with a daring plan.

She made not
one building but a set of three,
split into fragments that weaved the
setting together.

The structures
weren't just
beautiful — they
made everything
around them more
beautiful, too.

Zaha's next big goal was to design a project in the United States. She was waiting for the perfect opportunity, and it finally arrived: a competition for an art museum in Ohio. Zaha designed the galleries to look like a stack of concrete boxes floating on air. It was no contest! Zaha's winning proposal made her the first woman to ever design a museum in the United States. And artists were so inspired that they even began to make art specifically for the museum she designed.

Zaha was finally building momentum. Clients clamored to hire her, fellow architects studied her designs, and students dreamed of working in her studio. Zaha would throw her colorful silks and jangling jewelry into a suitcase and take off for France, Singapore, or China to work on projects — sometimes at a moment's notice.

All over the world people stopped to stare
at the shapes and structures she had created.

ZAHA HADID

She now had hundreds of buildings
to her name, and thousands of people
lined up to see exhibitions of her work in
Vienna and New York. Zaha became the
youngest person to win the Pritzker Prize,
the highest award an architect can receive.

No matter where her projects were, Zaha always tried to achieve two goals. One was harmony between humans and their surroundings. The other was a sense of change, movement, and never standing still. Was she remembering her adventures in the Sumerian marshes? Or the intricate light and shadow play in the mosques and palaces of Baghdad? Zaha smiled: she would never explain why her buildings looked the way they did. They would speak for themselves.

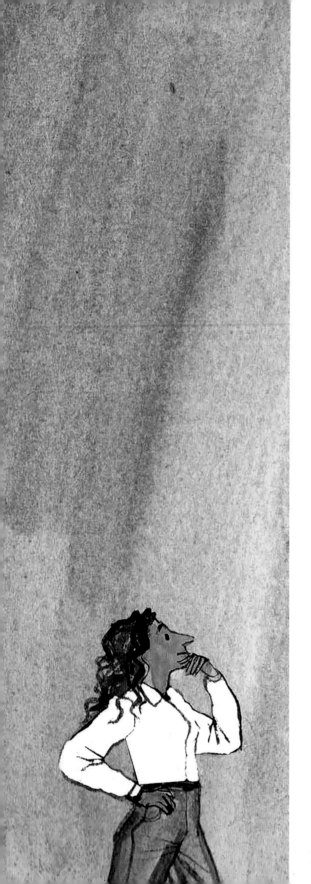

Author's Note

I started drawing houses at age two — with oddly shaped roofs, round walls, or too many windows to count. I loved drawing those houses and writing stories for the people and animals who lived in them. When I learned I could make a career out of this my goals were set. When my family emigrated from Russia to New York in 1992, I started architecture school. I learned that architecture is more than beautifully drawing buildings — good design identifies problems and offers solutions. This made architecture sometimes feel like math. I loved this, even though math wasn't my strongest suit.

I began to study modern architects all over the world — and Zaha in particular. At that time, Zaha was already well on her way to becoming a competition-winning machine. Watching her ideas become real was more than inspiring to me. It was a call to action. Zaha demonstrated to me, from afar . . .

- How to set yourself apart from the competition (she created evermore original and daring solutions; she always experimented, and never repeated herself).
- How to support and encourage your collaborators (her team labored together for years before seeing a project get built).
- How to persevere in a field that discriminates against women (even though her personality was fun-loving and warm, the press constantly described her as "scary" or "a diva"; the truth was, she had to be tougher than any male architect in order to succeed).
- How to embrace reinvention (she was an early digital pioneer and quickly recognized the opportunity and impact computing would have on architecture and construction technologies).

When Zaha passed away in 2016, she had an astonishing thirty-six projects underway. One of those projects is 520 West 28th Street in New York City, fondly known as the Zaha Hadid Building. I often stand on the sidewalk in front of it, getting lost in the mind-boggling geometry of the façade — so simple, and so complex. It's hard to take in the volume of the building from street level, so I climb the steps to the High Line, the elevated park that runs past it. I follow the interlocking window curves as I walk higher and closer. It's more than just a building to me, more than an important architectural project, or even a work of art. It's a question and an answer, a problem and a solution. It's impossible to imagine anything else in its place.

I wish Zaha could have seen it become a reality. But then again, she probably had, long before everyone else.

Selected Timeline

Zaha Hadid, 1956.

1950, October 31 — born in Baghdad, Iraq

1972 — receives degree in mathematics at the American University of Beirut and moves to London, England, to start school at the Architectural Association

1977 — graduates university with the Diploma Prize and starts work under professors Rem Koolhaas and Elia Zenghelis at the Office for Metropolitan Architecture in Rotterdam, the Netherlands

1980 — leaves to start her own firm, Zaha Hadid Architects, in London, England

1982 — wins competition for The Peak hotel and sports club in Hong Kong, marking her debut into the limelight as a formidable architect despite it never being built

1990-1993 — designs the Vitra Fire Station, her first successfully realized project, in Weil am Rhein, Germany

1994–2006 — designs the Spittelau Viaducts Housing Project in Vienna, Austria

1997–2003 — wins competition for the Lois & Richard Rosenthal Center for Contemporary Art in Cincinnati, Ohio, making her the first woman to design a museum in the United States

2004 — awarded the Pritzker Architecture Prize, becoming the first woman, first Iraqi, first Muslim, and youngest person ever to receive this honor

2006 — a thirty-year retrospective of Zaha's work is exhibited at the Guggenheim Museum in New York, United States

2012 — receives the honorific title Dame Commander of the Order of the British Empire

2016, March 31 — dies in Florida, United States

Dame Zaha Hadid in her London office, 2011 (above) and at the opening of the Stuart Weitzman Flagship Store, which she designed, in Hong Kong, 2014 (below).

Selected Bibliography

Betsky, Aaron. *The Complete Zaha Hadid*. London: Thames & Hudson, 2016.

Giovannini, Joseph. "In Memoriam: Zaha Hadid, Friend." *Architect Magazine*. April 1, 2016.
    https://www.architectmagazine.com/design/zaha-hadid-friend_0.

Highfield, Roger. "Zaha Hadid on Maths, Architecture, and Women in Science." Science Museum. October 14, 2014.
    blog.sciencemuseum.org.uk/zaha-hadid-on-maths-architecture-and-women-in-science.

Lewis, Anna M. *Women of Steel and Stone: 22 Inspirational Architects, Engineers, and Landscape Designers*.
    Chicago: Chicago Review Press, 2014.

"'Would they call me a diva if I were a guy?' Zaha Hadid, Architect and Woman." April 11, 2016.
    moazedi.blogspot.com/2016/04/would-they-call-me-diva-if-i-were-guy.html.

https://www.theartstory.org/artist/hadid-zaha/life-and-legacy/

https://www.zaha-hadid.com/architecture

To my parents,

whose curiosity and

creativity shaped me.

And to Zaha, for being a bright light. – V.T.-K.

Thank you Rosa Sheng and Dahlia Petrus for their expert reads.

Photo captions and ©: **front endpapers:** left: Evelyn Grace Academy, London, England; Luke Hayes-VIEW/Alamy Stock Photo, left top: Port House, Antwerp, Belgium; Tony Vingerhoets/Alamy Stock Photo, left center: Heydar Aliyev Centre, Baku, Azerbaijan; Zaha Hadid Architects, left bottom: concept art for The Peak Leisure Club, Hong Kong, China; Zaha Hadid Foundation, right center: Heydar Aliyev Centre, Baku, Azerbaijan; Hufton+Crow-VIEW/Alamy Stock Photo, right: Lois & Richard Rosenthal Center for Contemporary Art, Cincinnati, USA; Arcaid Images/Alamy Stock Photo; **timeline:** top: Zaha Hadid Foundation, center: Nick Moore/Alamy Stock Photo, bottom: Jessica Hromas/Getty Images; **back endpapers:** left center: Vitra Fire Station, Weil am Rhein, Germany; Geoffrey Taunton/Alamy Stock Photo, left bottom: Spittelau Viaducts Housing Project, Vienna, Austria; Viennaslide/Alamy Stock Photo, right center: 520 West 28th, New York, USA; David Whitestone/Alamy Stock Photo, right top: Galaxy SOHO, Beijing, China; Imaginechina Limited/Alamy Stock Photo.